What Is Fascism

Sergio Panunzio

Translated by Richard Robinson

Sunny Lou Publishing Company
Portland, Oregon, USA
http://www.sunnyloupublishing.com

Corrected: 2025 September 13
Original Publication Date: 2025 August 25

ISBN: 978-1-955392-79-2

This translation from Italian is based on the
Alpes, Casa Editrice edition of
Che cos'è il fascismo, Milan, 1924.

Contents

Translator's Preface

This will be the third book on Italian politics that I have translated, and I have to admit that the more I learn about Italian politics from the latter half of the 19th century to the first half of the 20th – that is, from the Risorgimento to the end of WWII, – but really, more specifically, about that formative time in Italian politics, during the first quarter of the 20th century – the more fascinated and interested I become.

Fascism is, today, one of those portmanteau words or, at best, equivocal terms, that means everything and its opposite, collectively, depending on who is speaking and to whom. Most of the time, as it is used today, it means nothing more than the worst insult one's generally radical Socialist, or left-leaning, opponent can hurl. I say hurl because it really is designed not so much to be accurate and stick as to stun and set off balance. Heard often enough, however, one becomes inured and immune to it. Heard more often still, one becomes curious. Ultimately, against one's opponents' "best" intentions, one may even own it. It won't be the first time in the history of the world that what was originally meant to be a slur was later worn like a badge of honor. Cynicism comes to mind, and later Decadentism.

Sergio Panunzio is one of the leading and first ideologues of Fascism, and even he has difficulty, as the reader will discover, in defining the term. Although he makes a good attempt at it and we find it useful.

As for Panunzio himself, it is surprising how important he was and is in the early formation of Fascism, and how little known he is outside Italy, if not inside it.

We hope that this translation and the ones that may follow it, will help correct the situation in the English-speaking world, in more ways than one, particularly politically. It is by studying and understanding the past that we can – in short order – make sense of the present and build a better future. At least, that is an intention.

– Richard Robinson, Edinburgh

Dedication

Ferrara, February 20, 1924.

Dear Crollalanza,[1]

Last August you invited me on behalf of the Fascist Federation of the Province of Bari, which you direct, to commemorate the March on Rome. I accepted your invitation. Having published now, in this small volume, the speech delivered by me on October 28, 1923, in Bari, I turn my thoughts immediately to you, and to the Fascists and syndicalists of my native province, to whom these pages are dedicated. When I accepted the invitation of my dear old friend Ciarlantini to write a small volume on political culture for the young publishing house "Alpes," I believed that it was fitting to make my speech available in print, to bring it to the awareness of a wider audience than what had filled Teatro Petruzzelli[2] on that unforgettable and solemn day in October.

With many warm regards, your most affectionate,

SERGIO PANUNZIO.

---

[1]Crollalanza: Araldo di Crollalanza (AD 1892 – 1986), an Italian journalist and politician. He led the Pugliese Squadristi in the March on Rome in 1922, and was elected mayor of Bari in 1926. In 1928 he was appointment State Secretary of Public Works under Mussolini.

[2]Teatro Petruzzelli: Petruzzelli Theater, the largest theater in Bari, Italy, and the fourth largest in Italy, which opened in AD 1903. It originally could seat as many of 2,192 people.

The March on Rome

The March on Rome

Introduction

Gentlemen!

One year ago, we were at the March on Rome. The whole Peninsula, in all the streets, from the peripheries to the center, was teeming, fantastically, with Blackshirts.

One year ago, the Blackshirts of Italy marched in columns on Rome, ready and resolute for anything, irrevocably. The triarii,[3] the organized masses of workers in the National Syndicates, firmly held the cities. We had already participated in the events at Ferrara, Rovigo, Bologna, the solemn gatherings at Udine, Cremona, Milan, the assaults on Bolzano and Trento.

One year ago, H. M. the King of Italy summoned Benito Mussolini, the Supreme Leader of Fascism, to assume leadership of the Government of the State.

Gentlemen, the date that we are commemorating today is not a political date, but a historical one. Fascism, upon entering the Capital, entered regally, incorporating itself into the history of Italy. And for

---

[3]*triari: Triarii* (or "third in line") were heavily-armed veteran soldiers, forming the third or last line of the army during the early Roman Republic.

this reason, today's celebration is at one and the same time the celebration of a [Political] Party, our glorious Party, which has given three thousand dead to the cause, and to whom, reverent, emotional, and silent, we give in return, first and foremost, our grateful salute – but it is also a celebration of the entire Nation.

The act was immediate, genial, overwhelming. Above all, because it was necessary. The time was ripe. The iron was hot. Italy did not have a government. Mussolini saw, came, conquered. It is recounted – and the episode is perhaps filled with more human and dramatic significance than the entire brief and rapid scene – that no sooner had Il Duce, who found himself in Milan, put down the telephone which had conveyed to him through the offices of the General Cittadini the Sovereign's invitation to go to Rome, he had to exclaim, in pure Romagnol, to his brother who was standing beside him: "If only our father were alive..." That pensive man, pallid in face and with a heart hardened in battle and for battle, who had taken and assumed the whole responsibility of the history of the Italian people upon himself – even he, for one instant, succumbed to a flood of emotions while two big tears streamed down his cheeks. All this, o Gentlemen, is a beautiful thing, and it brings to mind, through a rich association of ideas, another episode, it too one of the most significant of all the historic days of the March on Rome: the tender episode of the Blackshirts who noticed, while returning from the Eternal City, at the train station in Florence, the Baron Sidney Sonnino leaning out of a small window of the wagon, and they shout out to the old Man their thunderous and generous *alalà!* – although he was on the threshold of death, his eyes at last were moist with the tears of great satisfaction and joy. Not missing from this scene of truly epic proportions was the participation of the ranks of young men, bold and brave, from our Puglia, and I can still see in the faces of the Blackshirts and the citizens of Upper Italy both wonderment and encouragement at the presence of the legendary Fascist cavalry of Puglia led by our heroic and intrepid Giuseppe Caradonna. It was the finishing touch to [an extraordinary] picture. Without the charm that emanates from myths, the masses, the great masses, are not moved, are not borne to supreme destinies, to the goal of sacrifice and glory. A new scene, never before seen in the more than one-millennial-old history of the Peninsula, without legal obligations or coercions, spontaneously and *en masse*, fifty thousand Blackshirts, from every province, speaking every dialect of Italy, had gathered, a few days before in a great moral and military review, in Naples. Italian history, and not just Italian history, had never known a cohesive army to emerge, almost stealthily, from the genius of the stirp, obedient to one single impulse, to one single law, to one single leader. It was the gathering of all Italy, the confluence of all voices, all histories, into one single history, one single, powerful, deep, and overwhelming voice, for the conquest of one ideal summit: Rome.

The Italian Revolution

The Italian Revolution, taken up again and led to its goal by Fascism, the Constitutional Revolution that founded the Italian National State, was and remains unique in the history of the world, as Il Duce declared on November 16 to the Chamber [of Deputies], because it was not stained – as other revolutions [were] – nor, in this respect, can the bloody Russian Revolution take any lessons, for all its wickedness and senseless slaughter, from the French Revolution with its crimes and innocent blood.

Many, at home and abroad, paled and trembled. Mussolini did not pale and did not tremble.

It was preordained. The Italian Revolution, culminating in the March on Rome, began in May 1915 with the intervention of Italy – desired and effected by a great Italian and fierce Pugliese: Antonio Salandra – in the world war. We can go further back [in time] and be more precise. The Italian Revolution begins the day on which, guided by Benito Mussolini, the first Fasci of Revolutionary Action[4] came out in support of the intervention in November 1914. It was written that Mussolini was to enter Rome in October 1922. The March on Rome solidifies and concludes the historical revolutionary period that had begun in November 1914.

"Revolutionary government" was what the

---

[4]Fasci of Revolutionary Action: (*Fasci d'Azione Rivoluzionaria* in Italian) a political movement founded in 1914 by Benito Mussolini.

Austrian Chancellor called the Salandra-Sonnino Government which emerged in the days of May. All of Italy's war was a revolution. Europe and the world feel it today. Mussolini tolerated, suffered, indescribably, the havoc of Vittorio Veneto,[5] which was the luminous sanction for the intervention. He was bound to take over the State – [which was] through [years of] decadent governments incapable of feeling and administering – and make it worthy, internally and externally, of Italy's victory. After the victories against the external enemy, the revolutionary effort was far from over, however. The final battles, unfortunately, were necessary, imposed on us, not wanted by us, against the internal enemy, against the old Italy [which was] not yet persuaded of its irrevocable death. Gabriele d'Annunzio, with a gesture of superhuman revolt, gave the first signal. Following the external war, we had civil war. More dead. More blood. How many more youthful victims, and not fallen in open battle even, but almost always in despicable ambushes. And to think that Mussolini had spoken to the House, making a profound impression: "The dead weigh on us, from whichever side." – In vain. Those who did not understand the intervention [of Italy in the war], did all they could and omitted nothing [in their power] to bring about its defeat – they had to sing the praises of Russian dissolution, to try to impede the fateful course and crowning moment of the Italian Revolution. In vain. Even in the darkest and most desperate moments of the autumn of 1919, when the Bolshevik orgy and dissoluteness reigned in the

---

[5]Vittorio Veneto: in reference to the Battle of Vittorio Veneto, between Austria-Hungary and Italy, which lasted from October 24 to November 3, 1918, and ended in victory for Italy.

streets, and the chests of our glorious soldiers and officers, covered in medals, were spat on, Benito Mussolini – with very few others – did not despair, but intuited – while encouraging and sustaining, at all costs, the morale of the younger and quivering Italian forces – the decisive day of his absolute triumph and the historical vengeance of the victorious and living Italy against the vanquished and defeated Italy.

After Piave[6] and Vittorio Veneto – memorable battles that decided the world war – Benito Mussolini had to come to Rome. It is to the name of Mussolini – Gentlemen, history is history – that the most recent events of Italy are tied. Reread the pages of the *Libro Verde* of May 1915 and you will see whether the Treaty of the Triple Alliance[7] would have been torn up and the intervention of Italy effectively brought to pass, if it weren't for Mussolini, the leader of Interventionism.[8] Mussolini, Leader of Interventionism, Leader of Fascism, Leader today of the National Government, the representative figure of the Italian Revolution, is not merely a physical person, but a moral person; he is the personification of Italy, he is Italy itself, which has suffered much, has shed much blood, but which trudges and trudges, trudges and works,

---

[6]Piave: more specifically, the Second Battle of the Piave River, fought between Austria-Hungary and Italy, June 15 through 23, 1918.

[7]Triple Alliance: an alliance between Germany, Austria-Hungary and Italy which was formed in secret in 1882 and ended in 1915 with Italy's entrance into World War I against Germany and Austria-Hungary.

[8]Interventionism: a movement advocating Italy's intervention in World War I, against Germany and Austria-Hungary.

works and trudges, to gain its law, to give, perchance, its law to other peoples.

Behold the Italian Revolution, and the historical significance of the March on Rome, decisive date and event in contemporary history.

The phrase "revolutionary war" – which refers to the war of the Entente against the Central Powers – has been much abused in the past. The truth is that if the war of Germany was a depredatory war of destruction and plunder, and the Anglo-French war, backed by Russia, was a war of preservation and profit, which usurped the reputation of the revolutionary war, then only our war, included purely for reasons of diplomatic contingency in the war of France, England and Russia, but autonomous and fiercely national, was revolutionary in essence, and indeed, more than a war, it was a great historical revolution.

The world is only now beginning to have a sense of this and understand it, because the hour of our past Hamlet-like governments, incapable of bearing the immense weight of the Italian Victory, is over; and there is, at the direction of the State, a National Government that derives the titles of its absolute, sacred, and intangible, but also moral and juridical, legitimacy – ennobled by the blood of hundreds upon hundreds of thousands of sons of Italy – from the indissolubly bound days of May 1915 and October 1922.

The National State

Italy is now complete, and it is inviolable. It is defined by its physical and moral borders. Without Fascism, the established borders in Giulia, Trento, and
Alto Adige were nothing but a juridical fiction. Italy
is a great nation, it now has a government worthy of
it, and it is becoming a State. Amid so much ruin and
so many wrecks, it is the most solid and robust State,
the granite cornerstone of European politics. Nor is it,
indeed, exaggerated to assert that all European life
will continue to gather round, as it has already gathered round, this active center of life and power, which
is Italy. This life, this vitality is no longer a generous
loan by others, but a real social and national substance, for itself and for others. In other words, it has
become a great Power, and for that reason it aims, as
is the law of all great statal formations, to have a
global policy, and not to suffer but to produce and to
establish the law and the laborious, crucial balance of
international relations. We have destroyed the calum-
nious legends and infamous rumors, against which all
our history cries out, from 1848 to '59 to '66 – when
the valor of our Italian soldier, was not ignored – at
Adwa, at Tripoli, at the Dardanelles – but was magnificently put to the test, even on the Amarissimo.[9] In
1867, a great French politicker, Adolphe Thiers,
speaking before the French Parliament, uttered these
unjust words: "The right of a people is founded on

---

[9]Amarissimo: Italian for "Most Bitter." It is in reference to the
Adriatic Sea, after to a line by Gabriele d'Annunzio –
"l'Amarissimo Adriatico" – with an allusion to the Austrian
domination on the eastern coast of the Adriatic.

their blood. But the Italians have founded their right on the blood of others." I find these words quoted in an ardent speech made on November 2, 1881[10] by a precursor of Italian Nationalism and a companion of Francesco Crispi, Rocco De Zerbi.

These words have definitively been erased. Italy exists. Everyone respects us. Better is it, in international politics, to be respected than loved. If we have Italy, we have a great task, which is, then, the historical and substantive task of Fascism, that of *creating the State*. Fascism is the true foundation and creation of the State. Fascism has arisen with the vocation, with the instinct of the State, because it is power, not destruction; order, not disorder; law, not anarchy; discipline, not Piedigrottesque[11] merrymaking. It is not the provinces, the cities, the campaniles that command Rome, but Rome that commands them all. For decades and decades, there were provinces in Italy in which the symbols, and only the symbols, of the State existed merely to be cursed and vilified. Today, no longer. The State is strong. The State of Fascism, the state toward which Italy is oriented, is the

[10]Original footnote: From the newspaper *Il Piccolo*, Naples, November 2, 1881. I reproduce here, in French, the words spoken by Thiers, as reported by R. De Zerbi: "*Le droit des peuples savez-vous sur quoi il se fonde? Sur leur sang! Et si les italiens avaient pur créér eux mêmes leur unité, alors, oh! alors je comprendrais l'orgueil avec lequel ils parlent de leur droit. Mais leur droit avec quoi l'ont-ils fondé? Avec le sang des autres!*" "Erase these words," exclaimed De Zerbi, "or let us prepare ourselves in such a way that we all consider ourselves ready to be able to erase them."

[11]*Piedigrottesque*: in reference to Piedigrotta, an area in the Chiaia quarter of Naples, well known for an annual festival that included merrymaking.

National State. By National State we mean an organic, powerful, animated, industrious State, well-organized in its rich and varied membership of classes organized into Syndicates and Syndical Corporations, and, above all, ruled by this hierarchy. The completed and finished statue does not yet exist; but the material is there; the form takes shape and is being worked out. Today, it is not admissible that only the Army should be hierarchical – the social and historical reality in which and by which we live, the world over, is essentially, like it or not, *military* – but the entire State is a great Army, a great discipline, a living hierarchy. A military Army alone is no longer enough; what is needed, bound closely with the first, is a greater civil Army, from functionaries to citizens, from citizens to functionaries. Not only are the soldiers soldiers and combatants, but all citizens, from the lowest to the highest, are soldiers and combatants, and the right, even that ancestral one of property, is no longer understood, let's be clear, as merely a private right, but as a duty and civic function; we are all living instruments of that symphony, very Beethoven like, which is national life.

The political form of this State is, it too, settled, and not by chance or caprice, but, in historical terms, for profound and logical historical reasons: It is the Monarchy, no longer parliamentary, liberal, pseudo-socialist, but the National Monarchy. When, in the quivering spring of 1915, Benito Mussolini posed the memorable dilemma: "Either war or the crown," and Vittorio Emanuele III, the valorous Soldier King, led Italy beyond its borders, the historic problem of what form of government Italy was to have, had already been resolved; in such a manner that, when Mussolini, presenting himself last year before the Sovereign who, mindful and conscious of the history of Italy, had summoned him, uttered the words: "Majesty, I bring to you the Italy of Vittorio Veneto," he was only continuing the speech of 1915, having removed only one term from the dilemma and, in doing so, historically sanctioned his devout homage to the crown. All that is crystal clear, simple, logical like a syllogism.

The State, irrevocably sanctioned by the March on Rome, is, and continues to remain, necessarily Fascist, and must attentively and constantly look over its shoulder inasmuch as it has emerged armed from the live and bloody womb of Fascism, like Minerva armed from the head of Jove. Every regime born of a revolution has the right, less for its own sake than in the eyes of history, to conserve itself, to consolidate itself. Otherwise, the life of the State would be child's play and political hysteria. The sculptor does not abandon to another artist, before having finished it, the statue made by his own hands, nor the painter the canvas. The creature carries within itself, nor can it renounce it, its family name and given name, the civil status of its creator, in sum. And as more months pass, the truth of the formula announced by me last June is confirmed: "All power to Fascism, all responsibility to Fascism."[12] Our shoulders are strong enough to bear the weight. No compromises or insincere and dangerous collaborations. However, the March on Rome is not over, but continues; it is not a

---

[12]Original footnote: See, in this volume, my interview from May 1923, "All Power to Fascism."

past event, but a present act, a difficult, diuturnal conquest, not an comfortable, otiose possession, and we
have only one real and serious method of commemorating it, and that is to continue it with a pure spirit,
enflamed by the fire of the ideal, projecting it forward
like a living thing, not looking back at it, and carrying
it, in this way, to its logical, ineluctable develop-
ments. Continuation and prosecution, not commemo-
ration. The right to stop along the bitter and arduous
way, ever in ascent, does not exist. If the old tasks are
finished or nearly so, more serious and difficult ones,
new ones, will take their place. The March on Rome
is a daily occurrence; every act of government, every
organization in the country, every act of discipline,
every act of affirmation of power abroad is a harmo-
nious octave inserted into the great epic poem of the
genesis and constitution of the Italian National State,
which is the *ultimate essence* of Fascism; and which –
we would do well not to forget it – as Il Duce has always taught us and admonished us, is a means, not an
end.

What is Fascism

By saying that Fascism is the means, not the end, for
bringing about the greatness and power of Italy in the
world, I have defined for you what Fascism is – because today, since the evident rebirth of Thomism and
Scholasticism, it has become fashionable to ask for a
definition of our movement. It is accused of not hav-

ing a platform. *Felix culpa!*[13] It is not, believe me, for lack of platforms that the Socialist Party has made a fiasco throughout Europe! What are its platforms? Nothing. They are frigid and unreal intellectualistic constructions, and the more perfect and precise they are, the more contrived [they become]. Their logical potential and perfection is inversely proportional to their practical effectiveness and power. Platforms, in [political] parties, are an old story. Old Testament! After Bergson in Philosophy and Sorel in Sociology, we live by pragmatism. What is needed is the *epic*, the fantastic construction, the myth. Action, the state of the soul, psychology, movement, in short, is everything; the platform is practically worthless. Even Fascism, from [being] a movement between March 1919 and November 1921, became a party by mechanical political necessity, and it was given a schematic platform, which you can read about. But what would this platform be worth without the state of the soul, without the enthusiasm of Italian youth, without the myth of the glory and greatness of the Fatherland? The truth is, as I keep repeating, that the essential nature of Fascism – which, in this respect, forms part of the vast romantic movement of reaction against contemporaneous political and social philosophical pragmatism – is *institutional*. If we break down its living and creative synthesis and place it, for a moment, on the anatomical table for vivisection and analysis, Fascism is presented to us as an organic complex of institutions. Which essentially reduce to three: 1. Action

---

[13]Felix culpa: Latin for "Happy fault."

Squads;[14] 2. Syndicates; 3. Competency Groups.[15] These institutions must be integrated into the general constitution of the State, grafted onto and incorporated into the still vital parts of the old trunk, to give rise to an organic and concrete – not mechanical, abstract, or cerebral – new constitution, which might be the result, not of artificial deliberations by Assemblies, but of the real and natural process of social and political reality – and this is, today, the central effort and problem of Fascism. These institutions have had, in two distinct phases of development, two diverse aspects: an apparent astatual, parastatal, and anti-statal character *before* the March on Rome, in the period of battle and conquest; and a statal and legal character *after* the March, after Fascism had identified with the State and became, as it has become, the State.

The *Action Squads* immediately became, by a stroke of political genius, the "National Militia"; the *National Fascist Syndicates* tend to become – as I am firmly convinced, by both factual and legal necessity – the *sole* and *obligatory* "State Syndicates," possessing full juridical personality and responsibility, both personal and patrimonial, in private and public law; the *Competency Groups* represent already in miniature, as with all the organic political formations, the future "Counsels" or "Technical Parliaments," to which the political future of the Country is reserved, as H. E. Mussolini declared in the first program of March 1919, and in his latest parliamentary speech of July to the House. And that there is our program:

---

[14]Action Squads: *Squadre di Azione.*

[15]Competency Groups: *Gruppi di Competenza.*

clear, definite, concrete. You want formulas, expressions, and lotto numbers, but we present to you, we offer to you, facts, institutions rather, that – make good note of it – are not firm and static, bu aret, like all vital products sprouting from the subsoil of historical reality, dynamic and in full development.

One hears [talk] from many different quarters, but not always with good and commendable intentions about: *Revisionism*.

Careful now. There is little to revise; what needs to be worked on, and the most essential operation, I believe, of Fascism – and the new constitution, organic and hierarchical, of the Party, recently ratified by the *Grand Council,* bears witness to how much I assume here – lies less in a theoretical revision and definition than in a practical one, which consists in nothing more, in my modest opinion, than a wise task of connection and corresponding distinction between the old and new institutions, whereby, without confusion, substitutions, usurpations, and reciprocal sabotage, but rather by giving to Caesar what is Caesar's and to the central Government and its local organs, the Prefects, the supreme power, we arrive at a rule of cooperative cohabitation, and I would almost say of concrescence, of the new with the old. The Constitutional Reform, of which people speak, and which is truly the touchstone of the Fascist Revolution, is all there, not in the projects and statutory Charters. From institutions to Constitution. Not vice versa. The Constitution is merely the arrangement, the coordination, the synthesis, the "juridical" definition, in short, of the institutions.

National Syndicalism

But allow me to pause, briefly, in a more particular
way, on Syndicalism. I do not wish to treat of, but
simply to deliberate on, the topic. For this is neither
the occasion nor the hour to do so. On the other hand,
my ideas on this matter are well known.[16] I'm a syndi-
calist and for a long time now. I will also tell you this:
Syndicalism and Nationalism, these two superb Italian movements which precede, not follow, the Italian
and European war crisis, which found themselves,
and not by chance, fervidly united in the national war,
have formed and form the vital body and soul of Fascism, to the point where it is no exaggeration to define Fascism as a realized form of National Syndicalism, and the Fascist State as a National Syndical
State. But that said, I do not hesitate to put forward,
however paradoxical it may seem, and however as-
tonishing it may sound to you, this clear, explicit, categorical question: Syndicalism, even under the form
of National Syndicalism, is it or is it not necessary
and useful, is it or is it not good for Italy? You see
that I – who am considered and many times targeted,[17] as the logical and, that is, the juridical and for-

---

[16]Original footnote: See, among all my writings, the most recent
volume: *National and Syndical State*, Milan, Imperia Publishing,
1924.

[17]Original footnote: See in *Critica Fascista* (Rome, Year 1, 1923)
the articles by SILVIO GALLI, GIUSEPPE MICELI, and AUGUSTO DE
MARZANICH, which criticize my conception of the obligatory or
State Syndicate, even if not always from the same point of view,
and predominately from a juridical point of view, the first two, and
from a sociological one, the third. See, moreover, in *Battaglie
Sindacali* (Milan, 1923), many articles that criticize my concept

mal mind of Syndicalism – am submitting here not a superficial question of form, but a radical one of substance. I will respond. If Syndicalism is considered as a *means*, indeed, as a coefficient, and the most operative, of the production of national wealth, and as the organic, intelligent, and conscious discipline of production, as my friend Edmondo Rossoni, the very young leader of our movement never tires of saying, then it is useful and necessary; indeed, it is and will be the secret of the well-being and prosperity of the Fatherland; if Syndicalism, on the other hand, will withdraw into itself, delighting in its particularistic self-sufficiency and conceiving of itself as deaf and opaque, and consider itself an end in itself, not a means of production, but of coarctation and the clogging of national production, then it will not be useful or necessary, it will go against nature, that is, against the economy, which is the backbone of the people, and will be a great evil.

The historical, not juridical, problem of Syndicalism is a problem of organic and efficient organization and "corporation" of the productive economic forces: muscle, brain, capital. The capitalist classes, which were saved from Bolshevism, would do well to understand it and take heed. But Syndicalism succeeds Capitalism, and presupposes as antiquated, if not exhausted or extenuated, the surging and explosive force – almost always anarchic and mechanical – of the turbid forces of production. First comes creation, then discipline. First, the romantic life of riches, then the system, the classic arrangement of it. We are in agreement. And there is more. Italy does not

from the class-conscious point of view of Socialism.

find itself, like England or France, to have ever had the full experience of Capitalism, in order to correct it, temper it, discipline it, legalize it within the Syndicates. Just the opposite; taken as a whole, Italy has not had Capitalism; it is only now beginning to have it, and it is currently undergoing the febrile period of growth and production. If it is true that social and economic phenomena are related, in the last instance, as the good Prof. Gini maintains, to the biological phenomena of virility and the physical strength of race, than this period of growth corresponds to the surging and productive power of the Italian race, which is, consequently, the race of Fascism. So that now the question is raised whether Syndicalism can drive, favor, channel, direct the Nation's productive energy, or whether it impedes it, limits it, extenuates it, restrains it, diminishing, if not destroying, national production, and whether it is ahead of its time, premature and early, or whether its time is now or about to be. I confess, as all of us must acknowledge, that the situation is serious and arduous, much more serious than that of the juridical systematization of the Syndicates, which ultimately depends on no more than a show of force by the sovereignty of the State. But if, under the impetus and constraint of the National State and by capitalizing on the capitalist experiences – both positive and negative – of other peoples, by trusting in the future – not Russia, but Italy will give to the World the model of the new, concrete social constitution – [then] Syndicalism will be *national* in both substance and form, and, above all, it will take into account that the postulate, or rather, the axiom, of Fascism and fascistic Sociology is *production* and the augmentation of production. I do not doubt that Syndicalism, by organizing the classes, by disciplining the productive forces under the direction of the Sovereign State and the Law, and by promoting education and vocational instruction, will simultaneously create both the economic and the political power of Italy, which today cannot be conceived of as separate, not even for a second. Economy and Politics, Syndicates and the State, are today the inseparable and bilateral terms of a single relationship of life and power.

The central problem of Fascism and Italy – now that our public finances have been restored, our credit raised, and the moral and legal fiber of the country reconstituted (today let us say it, filled with pride and satisfaction: if everywhere people are working and producing; if enterprise is secure; if there are no more strikes; and there is a feeling of economic tranquility everywhere, – even if all this is not, and has not been, without serious sacrifices) – the central problem is and always continues to be an *economic* one. I say: let us build the house, the container, and within it let us develop and work at the productive economic forces, the contents. If the house is to have strong master walls, that is, if the National State is to be powerfully "armed" with a mighty, institutional *Economic Magistrature* of a technically judicial character (arbitration, even if obligatory, is not enough; it is an expression of voluntary jurisdiction, an organ of [interested] parties; it is not an expression of the Sovereignty of the State, an organ *supra partes)* for [managing] conflicts that are inevitable but also necessary and salutary (the strikes themselves, when they had a logic and were not hysterical movements, did

much good for the industrial and agricultural economic progress of Italy) among organized groups and social classes; and if it possesses a powerful domestic
armed force, which the National Militia or Blackshirts
could, in my opinion, provide the model and precon-
ditions of – and if anyone consults the most recent
history of economic agitations in all the European and
American states, my prediction will not seem so risky
or unfounded – the National State will be able not
only to inspire and drive forward, but also to domi-
nate, without being dominated, the modern forces of
production and to round the Cape of Tempests in the
life of the peoples, which is the economic life – and
the cape will be a cape, not of shipwrecks, but of the
victorious.

Italian Fascism has this historical task before
it and will fulfill it.

Three Hypotheses

Observation of the present economic and social reality of Italy suggests three hypotheses and solutions: 1.
Emigration abroad of the Italian human commodity;
2. Emigration of capital from abroad, I refer particularly to that from America, into Italy; 3. Breakthrough
on the part of Italy of everything that opposes its des-
tined development, its law of being, which is the law
of life.[18]

---

[18]Original footnote: See, in this volume, the article: "Breaking the
[Vicious] Cycle."

With respect to the first hypothesis, you know that Italian emigration, for a complex of causes, does not appear likely to resume its quantitative rhythm of the past. Instead, everything suggests that from now on emigration will be from small, select, qualified groups, not large masses of people, but rather [composed] of intellectuals, directors, technical leaders, of brains in short, and grey matter, not muscle. Qualitative, not quantitative, emigration towards the countries of Eastern Europe; aristocratic, not plebeian. Consequently, even allowing for a certain amount of emigration, the first hypothesis does not hold or at least it does not resolve.

American capital will, of course, be able to be invested, slowly and gradually, under a form of joint economic venture in our industries, even in Italy; and, as you know, behind the toasts exchanged last July between our Prime Minister and the United States Ambassador to Italy, this is [included] in the directives of both Governments; but, accustomed as it is to very high returns and interest [rates], it is not to be expected, and we should not delude ourselves into thinking, that it could [ever] be transplanted in bloc and emigrate to Italy.

We come to the third hypothesis. In Italy, we are many people, too many people actually; we are poor in raw materials, we have little opportunity to save and accumulate because we must also eat and live, and we have little capital. We must break the cycle that confines us like a cage and makes it impossible for us to deploy our admirable abilities and forces of labor and production. When there is talk of a

breakthrough, however, let there be no misunderstanding. Fascism is not a warmonger, it is, on the
contrary, the greatest and most sincere and most gen-
uine lover and defender of peace, as the facts demon-
strate, for itself and for others. It is, from the international point of view, a phenomenon of peace, not war.
Fascism is the heir, valorizer, and executor of the war
and of victory. That's it. The breakthrough does not
need to be done. It has already been done. And it was
grandiose. It happened on the Isonzo, with our soldiers, as early as May of 1915. It is not a matter of
waging new wars, but rather of preventing them, and
of realizing and utilizing those already waged and
won, whose results were wasted and compromised in-
ternationally, but not destroyed – for, as in nature, so
too in history and in politics, nothing that is produced
is destroyed, but everything is preserved, and woe to
the absent! – for a complex set of factors which out of
love for the fatherland we will not go into here,
though they are on everyone's lips, and by the cow-
ardly acts of unworthy governments that rose to power since time of Vittorio Veneto until the entrance of
the Blackshirts' march on Rome. The war and the
Victory and their historical, not political [or] diplomatic, results are revalorized, reassumed, embodied
by Benito Mussolini, whose Government was immediately defined – and they were also defined by Diaz
and Tahon de Revel, Fascists and combatants united
together – as the Government of war [was] waged,
fought, and won; the Government of Victory.

A Fourth Hypothesis

What remains, therefore, is a fourth hypothesis, which I consider the most correct and comprehensive: national discipline. If we are united, disciplined, internally strong, and if we know how to be content and not be seized with delusions of grandeur, we will prevail abroad, we will make the instruments of credit of Vittorio Veneto, still liquid and callable, bear fruit, and we will resolve our foreign policy, which is what dominates today and takes center stage in the history and evolution of peoples.

The Foreign Policy of Fascism

Gentlemen, either Italy will be imperial, or it will not – and when I say imperial I especially mean Eastern, and when I say imperialism I mean expansionism; that is, economic, commercial, cultural, spiritual imperialism; a civil, cordial, and amiable collaboration with Eastern peoples who are now waking up to life and who appear filled with mysterious unknowns, not the imperialism of square kilometers. The fruits of war, sanctioned in solemn, prearranged Treaties, and which were stolen from us through fraud, will be, must be, restored. *Gutta cavat lapidem*,[19] and even the hardest rock. Like it or not, Corfu is the first example of the new, dignified and active, Italian foreign poli-

---

[19]*Gutta cavat lapidem*: Latin for "a drop [of water] hollows out a stone."

cy. The Italian people, as a nation, felt it and applaud-
ed it with their eloquent, composed silence. Even the
famous, London-style League of Nations has softened
its tone toward us. Italy practices an *active* foreign
policy, is present everywhere, and, in spite of its very
small size, throws its weight around everywhere; it
many times strikes, and will strike, without respect
for interests and unjust positions that were once believed and are still believed untouchable. Italy practices a global foreign policy – it pleases me to affirm,
from Adriatic and eastern Bari – aiming for a real and
not pharisaical reconstruction and general pacification.

All that is less by men's design than by the
letter of the law of things, for it is always true that
history and politics proceed from the encounter with
objective forces, and among these are, first and foremost, the geographical and subjective ones.

It is not without profound motive that Kemal
Pasià, the hero of the Turkish national reawakening,
broke through a major obstacle on practically the
same day that Benito Mussolini, the hero of the Italian national reawakening, at the head of the Blackshirts, entered Rome. It seemed that the East, especially the Balkans, was bound to burst into flames at
any moment. Who knew what they had to fear from
Fascism. The European Capitals were more than
alarmed – [they were] white with fear. And yet, [in]
experimental confirmation of the historical principle
that Italy, after Vittorio Veneto, is now the "lynch
pin" of all European life, especially the central, south-
ern and eastern parts, in short, of the Mediterranean,

[as if] by magic the March on Rome provoked a *détente* throughout Europe and a sense of substance and settlement. With the March on Rome, the task of Fascism's domestic policies took second place, also because the Country marvelously responded to Il Duce's plan and spirit, and foreign policy took first place. Gentlemen, Fascism today is an international phenomenon, one of the most important international phenomena in world politics. What does this mean? It means that the Italy of Vittorio Veneto was a success, and now it wants to weigh, or weighs, in the reconstruction of international relations. I will say more: just as yesterday there were many incredulous people and supermen who smiled at Fascism, denying that it had the capability to conquer the State internally (whereas the more serious and less superficial observers thought otherwise), until the moment when they were convinced that Fascism had entered the Capital and become the new Italian State, so even today there are many superficial observers and skeptics who in the various European capitals smile while denying Fascism's international capacity and potential. Short-sighted people, and they will realize it, just as our anti-Fascists have realized it. But those who go deeper into things do not think this way, those who already know that one must reckon and come to terms with Fascism in order to have a good and long-lasting friendship, and clear, very clear, pacts.

It was not Italy that jeopardized European peace – rest assured, Lord Grey – with its intimation to Greece, nor Italy that ruined the League of Nations; the peace and the League were poorly conceived and lifeless in Paris, because in the sinister year of 1919 the diplomatic vitality of Italy was next to nothing and calculations were being made and shaky edifices constructed without us and against us. And this is why Fascism, which is the resumption of Italy's diplomatic power, is considered – while, we repeat, it is the only true friend of European peace (and a single year of Government more than proves it) – a meddler and is targeted, perhaps while assisting certain unworthy, so-called Italian "refugees," by all the hack reporters and newspapers in the service of Geneva-ism, pacifism, and world plutocracy.

Mediterranean Resurgence

And yet, the things of the world, and of the Eastern world, get along fashionably, so that there is need of Italy and the forces of Italy. Italy has an international mission. And yet, if we want to avoid – *quod deus avertat*[20] – the "Balkanization" of the Middle East, after that of Eastern Europe, I think that it may indeed be true that England has more need of Italy than Italy of England. A system of *realistic* Mediterranean and Eastern agreements is, I believe, necessary between Italy and England, nor did Lloyd George himself, slyly reciting a kind of *mea culpa* at the Genoa Conference, even before Fascism's advent to power, fail to mention the absolute democratic and economic necessities of Italy and the means, without however specifying them, of their repair. The map of the economic and commercial policy of Eastern Europe has need of

---

[20]*quod deus avertat*: Latin for "may God forfend."

revision and correction. This revision must benefit Italy particularly.

We have – by now it has become a common-place – demographic surpluses and entire armies of labor; we lack raw materials; above and beyond emigration, we have need of colonization, spheres of influence, and markets in which to collocate our man-power, the products of our industry and agriculture. If Italy were located in Northern Europe, apart from the capacities of its people, it could also be sidelined in the economy of the new world, which has the Mediterranean as its center. Instead, Italy finds itself at the center of this sea, at the strategic confluence of all the world's commercial and economic routes and global trade. Also, even if it were absent intentionally, morally – and by this time it is not, because it is also very vigilant and alert and stands guard – it would still be materially present.

Geography is not an opinion or an invention, nor can it be discarded or thrown into the wastebasket of just any baize-covered table of diplomacy. The great modern role of the Mediterranean was conceived by Germany, which wanted to impose itself on and abrogate the laws of nature, by transporting itself – subjugating and making a *tabula rasa* of Italy – from the cold and frozen seas of the North to the warm and luminous Mediterranean seas, to as far as the Tyrrhenian, Ionian, Adriatic, and Aegean. What was unnatural for the German people – apart from the negative virtues and traits of those who have always remained militaristic through their global expansion – is natural for Italy.

The surest sign of modern times – we must go back to the end of the last century and to the beginning of the new one – is the rapid expansion of Europe, because of the increase in population, into extra European countries. Modern war is the war of continents, peoples, races. Our history deals with far more serious matters than domestic class warfare and... than petty provincial squabbles. The Asian continent and the black continent are the stakes of global conflict. Open an atlas from 40 years ago. Africa was a blank map. Open an atlas today. And to think that it was only in 1837 when the first transatlantic ship furrowed the ocean! The East returns, o Gentlemen, to the world stage, and it is for this intimate reason that the profound vocation of Fascism turns more toward the East than toward the West, and it explains the national love, I want to say predilection, of Fascism for the Mezzogiorno, and, allow me to say it, the ardent yet distant passion of Mussolini for Puglia and for Bari, which stand as the vanguard of the Italian Nation toward the East.

The resurgence of the East and of the Mediterranean, through the valorization of North and South Africa, through the creation of the Suez Canal, through the links of Europe to the Far East, has a magnificent signification: the return of human civilization to its origins. The Hebraic world, the Arabic world, the Indies themselves are in motion. Grave, silent, and mysterious Asia is making itself heard. "There are more things in heaven and earth than are dreamt of" – said the greatest English tragedian. Our local and regional problems are not the only ones in the world. There are great and terrifying problems shaking the world. And in the Far East and China signs of a national reawakening are appearing.

Russian Bolshevism itself has the Far East in its sights now. At this very moment, we are witnessing two synchronous movements: The West which wants to become more Oriental, and the East which, in its own way, while maintaining its national, mental, religious structure, whence the rising up of Asiatic nationalism, wants to become more Western. The Mediterranean is the age-old sea in which the West and the East, under the auspices of Italy, having become imperial again, must celebrate their fatidic union.

The Mediterranean returns to being the cradle of human civilization, and Italy, which is the firstborn child of the Mediterranean, must follow and favor the movement of rebirth in the European and Asiatic East. Not from America, where European civilization has grown but become only quantitatively exaggerated, but rather from Asia, the historic world of Nations may very well receive a new spiritual imprint.

In the magnanimous and multianimous Mediterranean, which witnessed the wealth and power of Italy across many centuries, not in the Atlantic, which saw the poverty and rags of our masses, a new human civilization is being forged. The greatness and power of Italy is framed within this historic resurgence of the Mediterranean and the East. Italy is bound to the East; when the East declines, Italy declines; and when the East is great, Italy is great. Consult the history of Rome. It isn't by chance that Italians greet each other today with the Roman salute.

Consult the history of the Middle Ages. When the axis of civilization shifts from the South and East toward the North and West, ending Italy's historical maritime mediatory role, the greatness of Italy is eclipsed. With the dawn of modern history, the Americo-Occidental mirage succeeds the Asiatic-Oriental one, and the countries of the South, meridional Italy among them, remain excluded, cut off from the traffic and global circulation of wealth and power. We, the ancient rulers, are reduced to living on the margins of others' riches. Hence, the unquestioned primacy of septentrional Europe over the Meridional. States, Continents, and Countries are mere creations of history, points of intersection along the routes of civilization. Today, the old balance is broken and the axis of civilization has shifted. We are witnessing the rotational movement of civilization from the West to the East; the point of transit, an almost immense wharf jutting out into its threefold roaring sea and stretched between two worlds, [is] Italy, this little spit of land which in physical area can barely be seen when looking at an atlas! The absolute primacy of Northern Europe, of the Nordic seas, of the Atlantic Ocean, is exhausted. It is pointless for England to concentrate its entire fleet in the Mediterranean. Today, the countries and peoples of the Mezzogiorno and the fascinating prehistoric Mediterranean regain their prestige. It is the wheel of fortune!

The European potentates must needs be convinced of it. The order and distribution of global relations and forces have changed. It is up to the Italian people with its discipline and with its sense of moderation and obedience to rise to the task of the hour and

to assist the work of the National Government, armed
with a strong Army, a powerful Navy, and a mighty
Air Force.

The Italian people lack none of the qualities
for being a leading nation in the world, worthy of the
historic moment that we are passing through. It has a
national thought, which it must spread through its
Universities, especially through the Adriatic
Athenaeum of Bari; it has an active intelligence; an
incomparably large workforce and will; it has given
luminous proofs of itself in the world war by sea, by
land, by air; it must be – and this is a point of capital
importance whenever one speaks about Italian empire
and imperialism – parsimonious, frugal, modest in
consumption, in enjoyments, in pleasures, because
without moderation greatness does not ensue – let
Japan today and Rome yesterday instruct us – there is
no point in making constant rhetorical appeals to our
ancient Roman fathers and to their Empire if we do
not seek to imitate them – not in luxury and deca-
dence, but in moderation and parsimony. We are
small, keep in mind this little spit of land; we will be
great, if we do not act like megalomaniacs, but if we
are strong and aware. The Italian people, who possess
all the virtues to realize its national and global role,
had need of one thing alone: to be *directed*, to have an
ideal and material direction; and it has found that direction in Fascism, true bearer and titular of the imperial greatness of Italy, which is emerging, between
West and East, from the cerulean, foaming waves of
the Mediterranean.

Fascist Italy will either be imperial, or rather,

oriental, or it will not be. It must exert – with thought, culture, commerce, trade, navigation – its influence on the Eastern peoples, winning their friendship and conquering them in this manner, not by iron and fire, not with the blows of banknotes, because people are souls not merchandise, [they are] spirits and ideal personalities – and the selfsame historic climate of expansion and colonialism has, it too, changed.

The Italians are not Atlantic or Pacific Ocean peoples, but Mediterraneans. The Blackshirts, who are already protecting the Confines in Giulia, and holding Tripoli in Africa, are not local, provincial, or regional peoples, but Mediterraneans. And let us remember it well, the same Adriatic that breathes at several meters away from us, which has so fascinated us, and fascinates us, the small, the closed Adriatic, is not an end in itself, but a passageway to the Mediterranean, and if we are Adriatic peoples it is because we are Mediterraneans, to the effect that we do not see any economic and political discontinuity between Bari and Trieste, Catania, Palermo and Naples, between Leghorn and Ancona, between Genoa and Venice, between Zara, Tripoli and Rodi; and when we speak of Italian imperialism to another person we do not mean anything other than the Mediterranean Primacy of Italy. Thalassocracy... that is the word written in indelible characters in our history and in our prehistory!

Conclusion

Gentlemen,

I have finished, and I thank you for the attention that you have been willing to accord me. But I cannot take my leave without first turning my thoughts to the Man who directs the destinies of the Nation. It is not enough merely to say – as if to get it over with: "It's Mussolini." No. We must all of us assist in every way, and with the greatest and purest feeling for the Fatherland, the fated man who leads the National Government. Let us all assist Mussolini and tirelessly work with him. While we are here, on a day of glory and triumph, solemnly commemorating – and all Italy is gathered together for the same reason in the theaters and piazzas – the event of the March on Rome, Europe is passing through a most difficult quarter of an hour, and there are States that first aroused fear and reverential awe in us, which [now] debate among themselves in a terrible crisis of disintegration and secession.

Let us turn our thoughts to our Heroes, to our Combatants, to the Mothers and Widows of the Fallen, to our glorious Mutilated, but above all let us remember our Dead, *all* the Dead, all connected together in the precipices and unfathomable abysses of death and in the evergreen jubilation of that great enchantress, Life. It is not true that the Dead are dead. They too, the Dead, think, and, as the greatest English poet says, they have, in the grave, their eyes wide open and dream; and they dream about what was, and what is, and what shall be; about sunsets and dawns;

about the past, the present, and the future of Italy.

We, the surviving generation, are as if gripped in a vise by two claims: by the claim of our Dead, by the claim of our little ones who, like the blond color of golden harvests in our approaching spring which invades the fields and already inundates and invades our streets.

> *Youth, Youth,*
> *Springtime of Beauty...*

All Power to Fascism

All Power to Fascism

"What do you think of the current political situation?"

"It's a bit difficult to say. But I will give you a quick summary. First, however, I need to make one thing clear. The Fascist revolution has had, since the very beginning, an imponderable and hypocritical enemy, however imbellic: the daft preconception that the experiment is provisional and that its duration in power [will be] brief. It is a mad illusion, based on the eventual and residual political activity of the forces adverse to Fascism being squandered in onanistic and vain expectation. Magnificently, H. E. Mussolini said to the liberals, days ago, that 'successive phenomena, testamentary or legitimate, are out of the question.' Fascism can, and indeed must, go on, but it absolutely cannot finish; because it is embedded in the historical *humus* of Italy. Moreover, even after five years or more, the vanquished of Russian Bolshevism continue to *bother us*, asserting that the reign of Lenin, from one day to the next, must end. And to say that Bolshevism is madness, whereas Fascism is a realized historical idea! This most essential point having been clarified, our attention now falls on that other one: the revolution of October 1922 is the consolidation of the revolution of May 1915, and the Monarchy, [having] become *national* from *parliamentary* as a result of the war, far from diminishing, was constitutionally reinforced in the days of May 1915 and those of October 1922. The miserable pretenders to succession who pose as guardians of the Monarchy know this only too well, and they are Pharisees. The Monarchy – let us not forget the discourse by Benito Mussolini at Udine – is a given, an indisputable fact, an axiom. The further along Italy proceeds, the truer the famous statement by Francesco Crispi becomes: 'The Republic divides us, the Monarchy unites us.' I always remember the words of my late teacher Giorgio Arcoleo: 'Crispi was a Statesman because [he was] a revolutionary.'

"The Romagnol statesmen is of Crispi's [same] stock. We must not forget the discourse at Udine. Even of Mussolini, it must be said, with Arcoleo, that from a revolutionary he passed into being a statesman. The Monarchy, therefore, is not put into question by anyone. Terrible was – who did not see it? – Mussolini's travail between the Republic and the Monarchy; but the discourse at Udine, the Convention in Naples, the March on Rome are historical facts that cannot be erased. The soul of Mussolini is an essentially dolorous and pensive soul. But when Mussolini decides, he does not turn back. He is a pillar!

"In 1916, at a banquet, I toasted him as Prime Minster of the Italian State. Those around me smiled. Many more smiled when, in the *Gazzetta di Puglia* of last July, I wrote an article entitled: 'Mussolini's Moment.' The events have proven me right."

"And what can you tell me about the crisis of Fascism?"

"It is a natural, if not beneficial, phenomenon. You see? I always carry with me in my notebook [a copy of] Vilfredo Pareto's interview, from last April, on Fascism. The words of the greatest political writer alive are a gospel. No man, risen to power through revolution and with the inferno that was reigning in our Country, has given greater proof of moderation than Benito Mussolini. Firmness is what is needed now, and he is doing his utmost in this regard, especially against Fascists, [who are] unaware that Fascism today is the State. There remains the matter of constitutional reform, which, as Pareto says, we will see the genius of the Head of the Government weigh in on.

"It is essential, in my opinion, to bring *political* activity back into the Fascist party and to foster the development of the three *institutional* bodies that make up the particular character of Fascism: 1. *Syndicates*; 2. *Competency Groups*; 3. *National Militia*. If this last one – which my very dear Italo Balbo is working on, as entrusted [to him] by the President – becomes militarily disciplined; is reduced to that very aristocratic and numerically limited first draft; and is selected for reasons of culture and ability, the Nation will be in a state of normalcy, pacification, and freedom – strongly guaranteed, it goes without saying. Excellent and efficacious, it appears to me, is the work of the present Executive Junta of the party, a true dictatorial organ."

"But with respect to the reservations and objections made in certain circles and in anti-Fascist newspapers about the applicability of Military Code to the Volunteer Militia, what impression do you have?"

"They are the usual Pharisees. They do more harm to themselves than to Fascism. There is *Squadrismo*[21] and they shout "brigandage"; the Militia is going to be nationalized – as Balbo said in Milan – and they invoke, with seditious intent, the rights of man and of the citizen. I would think that what is most urgently needed is to present to Parliament, which is in session, the bill of the Militia and have it passed into law. Nothing more, nothing less. The illustrious General De Bono sees things correctly and is a great servant of the State."

"And what about electoral reform?"

"What do you want me to say? In principle, I do not deviate from my article 'Electoral Reform and Constitutional Reform,' published in the *Popolo d'Italia* last March 25. My formula is simple: having hardened the discipline, which matures, *all power to Fascism* and a very energetic reinforcement of all the powers of the State: prefects, heads of police, magistrature, and especially this: the army. When complete normalcy returns, the elections [return], whose platform must be the reformation of the constitution."

"And as for our Mezzogiorno?"

"Must I repeat what I have been writing for more than a year now in *La Gazzetta?* The Mezzo-

---

[21]Squadrismo: a socio-political phenomenon in Italy, starting in 1919, that consisted in the use of armed paramilitary forces or "action squads" whose intention was to intimidate and violently repress political adversaries.

giorno has no use for proportional [representation], the uninominal [district], the State ballot or other similar electoral-related stupidities. The Mezzogiorno has, above all, need of a strong Statal authority; and then credit, roads, irrigation, ports, railways, commercial treaties."

If Benito Mussolini were to announce that the deputies were going home, the *true*, very generous, and great people of the Mezzogiorno would gladly spend what coins they have on loud bursts of fireworks.

– *From* La Gazzetta delle Puglie, *27-V-1923.*

Breaking the [Vicious] Circle

Breaking the [Vicious] Circle

A few months ago in an article published in *Emigrazione* and several weeks later in a foreign policy note, I was drawing attention to the problem of emigration and more specifically to the necessity that Italy feels to see itself supported, in its production efforts, by American capital. One can imagine with what spirit I followed and emphasized the recent, highly important Italo-American demonstrations in the capital.

Responding to Ambassador Child, the Hon. Mussolini very opportunely and pragmatically thought it well to declare that "Italy would, with great satisfaction, see a passage opening up in the rather rigid meshes of the 'immigration bill,' allowing for an augmentation of its emigrant contingent in North America" and "would view with equal satisfaction the employment of American capital in Italian enterprises."

Several days have passed since these words were uttered, but it is fitting to return to them with a calm mind, because they are important beyond words and because they contain perhaps the real, actual, and not simply intentional, solution to the entire Italian problem; which, as everyone knows by now, is essentially economic and only economic.

First and foremost, let us fix our attention on one point. The point is this. Italy, alone, from within, cannot resolve its own problems. Italy must make all possible and impossible efforts – in the moral and political world, the word "impossible" is nonexistent – as the Fascist government and the current Minister of the Treasury are now doing, by putting the country on the path to restoration and, administratively and financially, by putting its house in order. The pain and suffering of this surgical, energetic, and ruthless work is grave and great, and yet it is being confronted and endured. But woe to us if we lose sight of this being above all a "method," and woe to us lest we substitute the method, which signifies the road, for the goal, or the means for the end. If art for art's sake is conceivable, economy for economy's sake is absolutely inconceivable. Besides, if the goal of the current regime of domestic austerity should be to reduce Italians to misery and kick them to the curb, our entire economic system – which already suffers from the automatic effects of the contraction of income among the popular and middle classes and from the reduction in wages and salaries – would set out blissfully on its way to die by tuberculosis.

Therefore, it is madness and stupidity to believe and to think that Italy can and should make its own "riches" all alone and by itself. Italy, with the current Government, can and must become an orderly, disciplined country, and a strong and animated State, but neither under the current Government, nor under any other Government, can it cease to be what it is by nature: a poor, very poor country, insufficient to the magnificent, vigorous, and exuberant population that it has, to miraculously become a rich one.

It is as clear as two and two make four that if we remain stuck within the circle of pain, hunger, and blood of our tragic economy, we will end up brutish like beasts locked in a cage.

This cannot be, however, and will not be the destiny of a great people like the Italian people, especially now that it has, in Fascism, found itself or, as the philosophers would say, its self-awareness. We are no longer living in the days when our leaders implored, especially from America, assistance and compassion in a humiliating and deplorable way, but we are now in such conditions that the Head of our Government, as one equal to another, treats of and discourses on the Italian problem with the diplomatic representative of the great transoceanic Republic!

The [vicious] circle must be broken. This is the fundamental point. This is the historical, dynamic-expansionist, or, to use a widely misunderstood word, the "imperial" meaning, of Fascism.

"Italy either will have a global foreign policy and exist, or it will not have a global foreign policy and will not exist."

There is much, even too much, talk of Rome and the Roman Empire, but Rome did not terminate at Piazza Colonna, it extended beyond the confines and beyond the seas.

Let us stop talking now about a total revision of the English and French Mediterranean positions. The time will come, and, while Sidney Sonnino's soul is still dark and mute with grief, the injustices committed will be redressed. The Italians, the Italian workers, need not be damned to suffer hunger, poverty, unemployment, and civil war in perpetuity – for the five meals a day of the Anglo-Saxon lords, bourgeois and proletariat, Unionists or Laborists. And as Virginio Gayda observed days ago in this same newspaper, the Italians too, like the Germans, the English, and the Americans, must come together, placing themselves with their initiatives and their work in the lands of meridional Russia, so as to colonize "sui generis" the great, boundless Muscovite land. Will we Italians, as always, play the part of simpletons, whereby we stand back with our mouths full of anti-Bolshevik curses while other peoples take initial steps, without stupid scruples and idiotic political preconceptions?

But the most direct and immediate way to break the [vicious] circle is not for now for "us" to throw the French-English Mediterranean world into disorder and point at Russia's map, which is problematic and certainly not to be resolved any time soon. Instead, we must turn as equals, as friends, gentlemanly, to the United States.

The American ambassador, in praising Fascism, has praised Italy, and in expounding the philosophy and psychology of Fascism, he has expounded the philosophy and psychology of Italy. A country like America cannot fail to be well disposed towards us. The fundamental secret of the life and power of peoples is their virility and physical strength. Peoples who have strong fists and know how to use them when needed, will sooner or later end by triumphing and by proving themselves right. The Americans, who are very distant from us, and who, for that reason, have nothing to fear from us, know this perfectly well. That is why they appreciate us and have a great deal of faith in our present and in our social and economic future.

But let us understand things well and properly. Even with America, two paths present themselves to us for breaking the [vicious] circle: either the flow of Italian manual labor into America thanks to emigration, or the flow of American capital into Italy to kick-start our industries and connect them with our enterprises in a bilateral and complementary system.

I do not have any illusions about the first path, and it is for that reason that I have deliberately emphasized the words of our Honorable Prime Minister, which allude to the second – that is, to the influx of American capital into Italy.

We must not close our eyes to reality. Today, things are what they are. In periods of peace and normalcy, emigration was a pacific and normal phenomenon. Not today. Emigration, in the historical climate of war in which we live, has lost its guise as an economic phenomenon, and has reassumed its primitive aspect of a bellicose or quasi-bellicose phenomenon. Fundamentally, what is emigration if not the movement of a people from a poor territory to a rich one, with the murder or, at the very least, with the expulsion or captivity of the people that inhabit the latter territory? The ultimate goal of Italian foreign policy is this: to spread out, for better or for worse, across the

world, in order to live and to work. And let us hope
that whoever still lacks judgment will mend his ways.
But do you believe that even America today is, as it
was yesterday, disposed to accept our pacific and economic emigration? Not in your wildest dreams. Before the end of the war, the Honorable Nitti, good
economist that he was, foresaw that the postbellum
commodity most in demand would be the labor force,
and that the labor market would eagerly seek Italian
manual labor. It does not seem to me that Italian emigration has picked up again to the levels seen before
the war. And if even America should have the tendency and perhaps even the "interest" in loosening the
mesh of the "immigration bill," we must never forget,
as I have shown on another occasion, that American
workers, with their strong Unions, will always prevent Italian workers, on entering into America, from
lowering their blessedly high wages – it has to do
with a true and proper war and, indeed, it is a return
to the primitive phase of the emigration phenomenon.
H. E. De Michelis, our Commissioner General of Emigration, after his recent visit to America, declared
having found "unanimous" approval for modification
of the restrictionist law, with the exception of Samuel
Gompers, who, for whoever does not know him, is
the head of the American Federation of Labor, and a
Second President of the Republic in terms of economic and political power. It is easier, I believe, to dis-
mantle bourgeois and capitalistic privileges than pro-
letarian ones.

In the important and most recent convention
of the Fascist Cooperation in Milan presided over by
our Postiglione, a courageous order of the day, pro-

posed by Engineer Fiori, was voted on – which makes me take back a little my profound, organic antipathies for the Cooperatives – in which a necessity was declared to transform "emigration" into the "expansion" of national labor abroad.

The idea is pure genius, and on it should be concentrated – other than on the electoral mechanism – the attention of all Italians, who, to be honest, will not exit the elections with their pockets full of coins. But without wishing to engage in pessimistic apriorism, where and how to find lands in which to expand with our well-furnished cooperatives, and [where and how] to place our labor abroad, if the lands are not ours or come into our possession, from those who hold them and have usurped them and fraudulently stolen them from us, [although] contested and denied?

All that remains, in my modest opinion, is for American capital, not only to break free from the stifling shackles and protectionism of unionized labor, but also to transmigrate a little into Italy, associating itself, among equals, with our enterprises, in order to proceed, united, in the conquest of real, "new" global markets, which are the markets of the European and Asiatic East.

If I remember correctly, last August, before the Fascist revolution, and when we still enjoyed in our country that blessed order that we all remember, our former Ambassador, Senator Rolandi Ricci, in a most notable interview with the Hon. Bottai, asserted that the American world of capital was prepared to send immediately to Italy about two hundred millions of dollars.

From August of last year until today, any progress?

Yes or no?

To these questions the coming events ought to provide an answer.

If Italy cannot go to America, let America come to Italy. Perhaps it is even better, for the one and for the other. A bit for both. America has already come to Italy once with its soldiers, or rather it had made an appearance. Let it come now with its capital.

– From *La Gazzetta delle Puglie,* 8-VII-1923.

Useless Formulas

Useless Formulas

The Hon. Baldesi is undoubtedly an acute writer who has often seen, and sees, things very clearly. Some time ago, I read his noteworthy article in *Giustizia*: "*Formula non viziata*" [Unspoilt Formula], which aspires to be the philosophy and theoretic justification of the most recent confederal attitudes. The article does not satisfy at all, inasmuch as it is based on a persistent and, I would say, almost deliberate misunderstanding of anything but a simplistic contemporary social reality. Before the war, theories [in general], including socialist theories, were able to guide action. Not to mention that the theoretical revisionism of Marxism (Bernstein, Sorel) had already made it clear, since 1900 and even before that, that the theoretical canons of pure and orthodox Marxism not only no longer served action, but were an impediment to it. But let us move on. Thought always moves forward, nor were the heretical revisionists of Socialism spared invectives, insults, and unfounded and foolish criticisms. One may also recall the very strong reflections [made] by Sorel against Marx's more obstinate apologist, K. Kautsky. Many people, in order to wake up and understand and accept the revisionist criticism of Socialism, had to wait to be crushed and maltreated in every sense and direction by the world war. Which was, in many respects, the transcription into realistic terms of the revisionists' prewar criticism of [socialist] theory and the indisputable confirmation of what the revisionists asserted concerning, for example, the infeasibility of (a) the universal proletarianization of society, (b) the reduction of enterprises to one type, and (c) the advent of a "single" and "unitary" program of production; and, above all, concerning the impossibility of a new, hypothesized socialist regime of production without a psychologically- and technically-prepared proletariat that was both educated and qualified. After the war, the socialist theories, already in crisis, and under water on every side, no longer served for anything, and to want to invoke them today in justification of actions, of certain practico-political actions, is out of place.

If the need for a new socialist doctrine was already felt before the war, what can be said after the war when "all" the conditions of European and global historical experience have been so radically altered and shifted? Baldesi replies that with respect to the socialist and confederal-syndical matter of finalism, any discussion is useless because "libraries are full of theories." Careful now. And what do these libraries say? They say that the so-called "scientific" socialism is more utopistic or, rather, more contradictory than the vituperated and superficially derided "utopistic" socialism. Some will remember, for example, the bitter and furious criticisms encountered in Italy, before 1900, by F.S. Merlino, whose socialism, while putting Marx in the attic somewhat, turned back to the utopists, to Mazzini, to [the ideas of] social cooperation, to justice, to the cultivation of the most profound and essential human sentiments, without excluding property, small property even, and did not admit the "unicity" of the antagonistic relationship between *a* bourgeoisie and *a* proletariat and even less dreamed of reducing society *en masse* to the proletariat without remainder, cancelling, upon pain of death, all the various multiple and growing social classes and ranks. Be very careful with the libraries, then. As for Fascism, which is, experimentally and formatively, the most integral and complex post-socialist and postbellum "social" doctrine, it is not yet formed and is even just at the beginning [stages], for Fascism marches in lock step with events; but already it is clear that, from the social side of things, it will critically summarize and assimilate the live part, that which is still alive, of Revisionism and of the Bernstein sort and the Sorel sort [of Socialism], creating something new, which cannot yet be defined and dogmatized. In many respects, the Fascistic criticism of Marxism (reaffirmation of small business, of small property, solidarity and the living synthesis in the State of classes, the empire of social unity and law) can be considered a transcription in terms of action, and of action many times violent and destructive, of Bernsteinian theoretical criticism, provided one recalls that the classical, philosophical, and highly serious Reformism of Bernstein, the greatest socialist thinker since Marx, has never had anything to do with parliamentarian ministerialism, abusively called Reformism, first in France, and later in Italy.

Leave Hon. Baldesi be, then, with his preconceived and prescribed theories. The essence of his reasoning is this: "I am a maximalist in finality and operate in the realm of dreams; as for the means, I am a minimalist and operate in and on present reality, which I cannot fail to be preoccupied with."

I have more than once pointed out the very se-

rious and politically ruinous error of dividing pro-
grams into maximum and minimum ones. We Fascists and syndical-Fascists are, in our own way, maximalists, because we adhere fully, and without mental
reservations, with eyes wide open, to the postbellum
reality that demands, at the risk of nullity, the Nation
as the minimum of "sociality" amidst the clash and
destructive medieval anarchy of classes and cate-
gories. What is Baldesi's dream? It is old socialism.
But is it still possible after the war to dream?

War is the point that one must never do without, because it is from war that a new experience begins, for better or for worse. It is amazing that Baldesi
can never be persuaded of this. Repeating the words,
which he calls "happy," of Georges Renard, he says
that the Syndicates aim, with a particular and realistic
criterion, at living conditions and labor conditions
that are superior ("superior," mind you, not "better")
to those existing, and, with a finalistic criterion, they
have grander ambitions insofar as they aim at the suppression of capitalistic ownership and wages and, if I
understand it rightly, at a pure and orthodox Marxist
type of socialization.

The suppression of ownership, of wages, and
socialization, are not frightening. The mind accepts
everything, and never fears anything. and must not
fear anything.

But, Hon. Baldesi, in what world do we live?
Has the proletariat demonstrated that it possesses the
qualitative, psychological, and political, not [to men-
tion] physical and mechanical, capacity to take over
ownership and abolish wages, and to socialize? No, it

has not. Revisionism had already said: The proletariat, as a unique class and as a unitary class, is a verbal expression, a declamatory formula. Even admitting the "existence" of "this" unitary proletariat, the proletariat cannot do anything because it does not know – such as it is – how to do anything; it knows, rather, only how to destroy (or rather to distribute), not how to produce. It is true, then, what the Marxists always said: Socialism is the very difficult matter of production, not distribution; but their actions were always directed at pumping – through the duties of the State, Municipalities, and Provinces, and from a myriad of parasitic, so-called new socio-economical Entities – money from the productive classes and at stifling enterprises by distributing high wages.

It is no longer permitted, with the trial by fire of the "historical" defeat of Socialism, a consequence of the incapacity of the proletariat, to dream or, what amounts to the same thing, to separate the minimum program ("technical" collaboration) from the maximum one ("political" collaboration).

Those today who do not wish to sleep must start everything from the top, by reconstructing the psychology of the productive classes. Nor should the not-yet-performed English Labourist experiment be cited, which, if it is performed, and according to the Marxist plan, will be a major disaster, worse than the Russian or Italian one. I remember discussing Syndicalism and the labor movement with Achille Loria in 1907 in Turin. The illustrious economist rightly observed that as long as the labor Syndicates carry out – with resistance and economic strikes, assuming even that they are directed at obtaining very high wages – a "quantitative" action, they will always remain at the most basic level of a capitalistic economy, without prejudice of the same. It is only if the action of the Syndicates became, with the strike and with the Sorelian moral pedagogy, "qualitative" could there be, as the Syndicalists said, a new regime of production.

In the first case, we have a "static" Syndicate; in the second, a "dynamic" Syndicate. What does the postbellum experience tell us? That the syndicates managed to wrest high wages, undermining production with their distributionistic-quantitative action, but they were unable to create a new type of production with a qualitative-productionistic action. And why is that? Because the proletariat has not shown itself to possess technical, economic, intellectual, and moral capacities, nor a "vision" or "general conception of life and the world." Baldesi says – it is a precious confession – that the social struggle must absolutely respect the mechanisms of a capitalistic economy "until they can be replaced, but it must aim instead at transforming the social machine in order to suppress the class struggle."

Let's forget about the suppression of the class struggle, which will never come to pass. But how exactly is the social machine to be transformed? Does Baldesi not see that our corporative or syndicalist-national conception is the greatest postbellum "effort" and "experiment" to give new bases to production? – I repeat: to production, not to the miserable quantitative and static distribution. And also, let's forget about the maximum and minimum program. Today, we must all be maximalists. Half measures are not acceptable. Either we reassert the old reality or we adhere to the new one, which is in the process of development.

Since this article has already gone on too long, I will say nothing, then, about how very little is represented today by the small matters of profit and wages and the petty internal class struggles – particular fancy and delight of old Socialism, including the confederal one – in the face of the vast and frightening national, imperial, international, continental, religious problems that Socialism has never understood and has never tried to gain a grasp of.

And so we come to the conclusion: It is not possible that the old system, having failed in the form of the Socialist Party, should be reborn under the more modern form of the Labor Party. The Labor Party is, at the point where we find ourselves, dead on arrival. For heaven's sake... but, to be fair, these things are no longer discussed anymore.

– From "La Gazzetta delle Puglie," *23-X-1923.*

Programmatic
Definition

Programmatic Definition

A "programmatic definition" of Fascism is invoked from many different quarters. The invocation is authoritatively made by my friend, the Hon. Bottai. The definition is necessary, but one needs to understand that more than a theoretic definition in the intellectualistic sense of the word, a practical definition is needed, in the political sense, or, rather, given that Fascism is a great social phenomenon [that has] entered into history, in the historical sense of the word.

I believe that I have indicated in this column, on another occasion, what seems [to be] the proper and essential character of Fascism. This is not a movement of merely anemic ideas, but a movement of real, robust, and corpulent facts. The organic unity of idea and fact, in history, is called an *institution*. It is not true that the institution is only a pale idea. It is not true that the institution is a mere and brutish fact, a fact whose living blood is the idea. The institution is a translated idea, alive in the fact, a fact whose living blood is the idea. Fascism, being an organic complex of institutions, its essential character, its definition, is to be an institutional movement. The institution is, socially, a free, spontaneous, instinctive fact, proceeding from the bottom up, whose dynamic law of development is the passage from the periphery to the center or, if you like, from Society to the State. The State is the highest all-inclusive institution, the organism, the synthesis, the constitution, one might say, of institutions, and their temperament. Fascism is a free, spontaneous, instinctive fact that has proceeded, in its brief, concise, rapid but also logical and dialectical historical development, from the bottom up, from the periphery to the center, from the provinces to the Capital, from Society, in sum, to the State. *From Institution to Constitution*, such, in synthesis, is the formula and personal equation of Fascism. In effect, in Fascism we find two clear and distinct phases: a necessarily institutional phase, inasmuch as Fascism *tended* toward forming a *new*, anti-statal State; a "constitutional" phase, inasmuch as Fascism itself has become the State. Just as matter craves form, so too institutions crave the State and are nothing but a great aspiration and original vocation to constitute the State.

Whoever recalls all the declarations by the Leader of Fascism will recall the truth of what is noted here. Since 1919, there has not been a speech, an article, a proclamation by the Leader of Fascism that did not clearly affirm the consciousness, the need, I would say the categorical imperative of Fascism, to be, to feel, to conceive, and to will itself to be a State. And if the touchstone of every historical movement is its attitude to becoming a State, it is indubitable that from the day on which Fascism conceived of itself as a movement tending toward the conquest of the State and toward becoming the State, Fascism resolved its internal historical problem and won.

It is not enough. I have already said on another occasion that seeing Fascism stretched out on the anatomical table, we find that it tidily presents, to a decisive critical analysis of its organic-institutional and compact unity, three technical formations or institutions: 1. Action Squads, 2. Syndicates; 3. Competency Groups. When people say that Fascism has not created anything and is without ideas, they close their eyes to reality, because they do not see that every one of these three institutions represents and incarnates an idea.

If, in the first phase of Fascism, which precedes the March on Rome, the three aforementioned institutions – and the first is more emphasized and emergent because of the necessity of combat – had a parastatal and anti-statal character, in the second phase – a realization of the instinct of Fascism to be and to become a State and to pass from *institution* to *constitution* – they immediately acquired a statal character, and, processually, of course, and naturally, [but] not without flaws, difficulties and obstacles, purely and without residual statal elements. The Action Squads immediately and ingeniously, in one stroke, became the legal force of the new State, and they were the first to actuate the transformation process, as they went from private squads to State Militia. The transformation of National Fascist Syndicates, from private-law Syndicates into public-law Syndicates, that is, unique, obligatory, or Statal – is in the process of implementation. The Competency Groups will not lag behind, over time, for they represent, from the institutional side, inasmuch as they involve the overturning or at least the radical correction of the old mechanical, electoral principle, the most personal and innovative part of Fascism, presenting themselves as the new politico-constitutional organs of the State, not just at the center, but also on the peripheries. Nor in the last great speech to the Chamber of Deputies did Benito Mussolini fail to observe that the near future holds, because Fascism is dialectical and proceeds in stages, a task of primary importance for the technical Council, or, rather, for the Groups.

Faced with this situation, I ask: In what must the requested and justly invoked programmatic definition of Fascism consist? The response for me is clear: It must consist, more than anything, in a wise and vetted work of connection and interpenetration, but also of exact and juridical distinction, of the institutions themselves, whereby one gives to Caesar what is Caesar's and arrives at, while avoiding redundancy, a normal and corresponding regulation of relations between institutions, and between new and old organs of the State. In summary, what is needed, in addition to analysis, is synthesis, coordination, orientation, and constitution of institutions.

There is talk (I'm pleased to cite our *Volt* for everyone's benefit) of constitutional reform, and rightly so. But reform must proceed from the innate movement of things, [and] must not be put before factual reality. If new organs know how to be grafted onto the old trunk – because the present historical movement is unfamiliar with the destructions that are mechanical operations belonging to the world of physics, but knows about the "creative synthesis" of [things] old and new, of tradition and innovation – and if, above all, they know how to utilize, connect, and constitutionalize new institutions, [then] constitutional reform will emerge alive and vital, fact and idea, idea and fact, from the things [themselves] and from the formative *nisus* of things, without the need to be deliberated on intellectualistically by an Assembly. The Assembly, if ever – as sometimes happens in all historical revolutions, actual, profound, and radical – will ratify the completed fact, by applying the final brushstroke.

The political programmatic definition that one feels the necessity of is therefore the definition – invoked by the Hon. Bottai – of the relationship between institutions and institutions and their [inter]connection, because if every institution goes its own way and obeys only itself, inasmuch as a *part*, and not the State, inasmuch as *the whole*, we will never have *one State*, but *three* or *more* States.

The unity of Fascism is historically provided by the unity of its Leader. It is to the leader, therefore, that the first initiatives are due, and it is He who represents, and concentrates, also by means of the Grand Council, the lively, unifying, and systematizing energy of the entire movement taken in all its varied and manifold unity.

About which, as about the Grand Council of Fascism, there is no room for discussion.

Let us talk, then, resolutely about the National Fascist Party. It is absurd, just as the distinction and contraposition between these two terms is absurd: Mussolini and Fascism. Mussolini is Mussolini because he created the Fasci and Fascism, and whoever consents to Mussolini and not to Fascism in truth does not consent to Mussolini either. Mussolinism and Fascism are one and the same thing. And therefore, the National Fascist Party must not only continue to exist, but it must also perfect itself, in my opinion, by reducing itself, aristocratizing itself, and consequently strengthening itself, because the most important hour of Fascism is precisely the one we are about to enter. Until now, the Fascist government has, in accordance with its commitment, restored peace, order, public safety to the Country, it has put the house of the State back in order, financially, administratively. A task more negative than positive, all things considered. The greatest tasks, new and positive, which are, then, the first and true accomplishments of the Italian National State, we have seen them in action in the area of foreign policy. And it is understood. Fascism, with the powerful National Militia, has morally reordered, and fortified, the country, and immediately recreated our great and glorious Army. But that is not enough. In the second year of the Fascist State, new tasks will present themselves, not so much reconstructive as constructive, and, therefore, for the establishment and realization of new political, social, and juridical directives of Italian life, the work of the National Fascist Party is more necessary and urgent than ever.

We have done the analysis above, noting that Fascism is resolved into three pieces: Militia, Syndicates, and Groups. But biology teaches us that life consists, not in pieces or analysis, but in synthesis and in the entirety of the diverse parts. The vital plasma, the genesis of the Squads, the Syndicates, and the Groups, has been the Fascio. This, the vital cell, the point of origin, the unificatory end of all and three of the parts of the movement. We must always be at the origin, we must never forget the origins. The Militia, the Syndicates, the Groups are formations, emanations, enucleations of the Fasci. The work of definition, of association, of which see above, depends on them – from periphery to center, from center to periphery – under the initiative of the Leader and the Head of the Government and his governing organs. This work, more than theoretical, is – I repeat – practical.

There will be a moment when the Fascio and the Fasci may reach their end – for Il Duce has always said and "warned" that Fascism is the means, not the end – and that moment will come when Fascism and State are no longer *two* terms, but will be totally, absolutely, and without remainder, *one* single thing: the Italian National State; even if today they are cooperating and converging. But this moment does not seem to me to have arrived, and it is absurd to think, for however rapid, close, and condensed the rhythm of Fascism's actualization and statal realization might be, that it could come any time soon.

We are in a period – let us use the customary phrase – of regular and full development.

– *From* "Il Popolo d'Italia," *9-IX-1923*.

The Double Aspect of Fascism

The Double Aspect of Fascism

I.

To define Fascism is not an easy matter. And it is precisely from this impossibility that many people draw the reason for their spiteful but negative and always superficial criticisms. However, after the triumphs and exuberant orgies of pragmatist philosophy, it should not be difficult for the class of intellectuals, critics, and hypercritics, to admit that a great historical movement, of national and international importance, can arise without the need for a precedently elaborate doctrine defined and expressed in a program. Fascism is, inasmuch as an idea, indefinable. It is an event that unfolds. To define it today, it seems to me, would be a *contradictio in adjecto*.[22] From this impossibility of definition and from the logical convenience of not looking for one, some people foolishly conclude that Fascism does not exist, or, rather, that it is neither real nor serious. We, on the contrary, will conclude with Goethe, that, since in the beginning there is no Word, but rather action, it is far better to stick with the facts and leave entirely to one side the intellectual – the "utopian," Sorel would have said – tradition whereby one must progress from doctrines to facts and institutions, whereas the facts and institutions are nothing without a point of logical, doctrinarian, and programmatic departure.

---

[22]*contradictio in adjecto*: Latin for "contradiction in terms."

II.

That is not sufficient. Fascism is insusceptible to definitions because it is a complex, very complex, movement that presents two fundamental aspects, distinctly opposed and simultaneous. Whence the fact that some people define it in a diametrically opposite way. The ones apply to it one label (let us say, for example, from the left), the others another (let us say from the right). There is not, in general, in life and thought, and, above all, in the social sciences, after Spencer and Pareto, a graver and more fatal error of simplism. The most serious obstacle to the comprehension of Fascism is precisely simplism.

III.

There exists, however, a social philosophy – an exclusively Italian glory – which, from the methodological point of view, may help to understand Fascism and to determine its historical value. This philosophy is contained in Vilfredo Pareto's sociology. Fascism may be considered, in large part, the experimental proof of this philosopher's doctrine, whose doctrines are based essentially on nonlogical actions and on the supremacy of the irrational in history.

What can be said, thus far, and with a certain precision, about Fascism is that it has to do with an Italian movement and, by consequence, [that it is] neither exportable nor comparable with other movements that have arisen in other places and at other times.

Fascism is a movement unto itself, original, atypical, of which there are not, and cannot be, any copies or imitations. Hence, its essentially historical nature. It is the product of two crises:

1. The general crisis of Socialism throughout Europe, made more acute in Italy by the economic and social conditions particular to our country, by the moral sensibility and rather keen political intelligence of the Italians. (It is not an exaggeration to assert that the most important product of European Marxist Revisionism has been Italian Syndicalism, in which G. Sorel rediscovered much of himself);

2. The crisis of war and post-war Italy, victorious in the war, but battered, until the day the Blackshirts entered Rome, during peacetime.

If one does not take into account these two crises, which are the true historical bases of Fascism, it is impossible to understand anything about the Fascist phenomenon. Which, as we have said, has two opposing aspects to it. This contradiction needs to be fully explained.

IV.

Fascism is, under a double aspect, both revolutionary and conservative. How and why? From this contradictory nature of Fascism arises the great difficulty of defining it; the stupefaction of pure conservatives and their diffidence in accepting it as a conservative phenomenon; the hesitation of revolutionaries in accepting it as a revolutionary phenomenon; the stupor in general, and the bewilderment in part, of [public] opinion – especially foreign public opinion – when faced with the indisputable majesty of the fact; and, finally, the inability to judge it in its nudity, or, what amounts to the same thing, the tendency to judge it with every sort of preconception, prejudice, or bias. In a word, is Fascism a revolution or a restoration? That is the main question. A question that, insignificant or nearly so in Italy, dominates public opinion abroad and, I believe, preoccupies it, especially in countries with a long history and rich culture. Of course, I am abstracting from the wretched defamations of Fascism made abroad by foreign journalists and publicists, and by our own compatriots transplanted or voluntarily exiled. It is necessary that criticism be made by critics, and not by defamers. It is evident that – roughly speaking – men and social classes are divided into two groups: conservatives and revolutionaries. The former, not considering but one aspect of Fascism, will spread the news that Fascism is conservative; the latter, not considering but the other aspect, as evident as the first, will preach and swear that Fascism is a revolution.

It would seem that the theory of the *double truth* is verified in this encounter: a thing is at once this and that, white and black! Eh, well, no; it is not like that. Fascism is neither solely conservation, nor solely revolution, but it is at the same time – under two different aspects, to be clear – both one thing *and* the other. If I may be allowed to use a phrase that is not empty of meaning, but is rather a dialectical conception, I will say that Fascism is a great "revolutionary conservation." It is what I wrote, if I may cite myself, in the *Popolo d'Italia*, the newspaper that Benito Mussolini founded in 1914, and which the history of the new Italy is intimately bound to. I wrote, in November, 1919, that it was necessary to *conserve*, from the past, in all the economic, familial, and political institutions, whatever cannot be destroyed without provoking the dissolution of the social body, not in this or that transient form of society, but in every society inasmuch as society; and that it was necessary to *destroy* all that cannot be conserved, by grafting new branches onto the age-old trunk, organically inserting the new into the old. One renews by conserving, conserves by innovating. These then are the two aspects of Fascism, apparently contradictory, but substantially united in one reality of thought, life, and history. That which constitutes the superb originality of the "Italian Revolution," that which makes it greatly superior to the French Revolution and to the Russian one is that, by reminding ourselves of and profiting from the teachings of [Giambattista] Vico, [Edmund] Burke, [Vincenzo] Cuoco, and all the historical critique of the Revolution of '89, it has conserved the past, realized the present, and oriented everything toward the future, within the bounds of historical conditionality and actuality. In certain respects, Fascism is ultra-conservative: for example, in its restoration of familial, religious, authoritarian, juridical values, [which had been] attacked and destroyed by the Encyclopedic, Enlightenment culture, which was arbitrarily transplanted even into the ideology of the proletariat, as much to say, into democratic socialism, which is the greatest culprit of contemporary corruption.[23] In other respects, Fascism is innovative, and to such a point that conservatives are frightened, as, for example, by its orientation toward the "syndical State" and by its demolition of the "parliamentary State."

We are contemporaries, therefore our judgement is poor. Conservatives find that Fascism is too revolutionary, revolutionaries accuse it of being too conservative. History will be the judge. History is unbiased. Whatever is visible in today – that which will stand out over time – is the *analysis* of the two tendencies, of those that today are already called the *two souls* of Fascism: the conservative soul and the revolutionary soul. The synthesis will come later, and whoever is alive then will see it.

V.

"The nature of things lies in their origin," our great G. B. Vico said. This principle practically explains the why and how of Fascism and its contingency.

It is necessary never to forget that Fascism is the unexpected outcome of two crises: that of Socialism, and that of the war in Italy.

During the fatal month of August 1914, the Italian Socialist Party, so as to be effectively, and not merely intentionally and verbally, revolutionary, ought to have been at one and the same time: fiercely

---

[23]Original footnote: See, in this respect, the profound book by AGOSTINO LANZILLO, of strong Sorelian inspiration: *La disfatta del socialismo*, 2nd ed. , 1918, Florence.

national and decisively *for the war*. It was neither the one nor the other, because its constitution did not permit it. Mussolini had immediately "intuited" this and abandoned the Socialist Party and, together with other subversives, founded and breathed new life into *revolutionary interventionism*.[24] Into this movement entered, for reasons of interventionist opportunity, numerous people of disparate ideas, many democratic among others, whose mentality (and that became clear later) not only had nothing in common with those of the subversives or revolutionaries – the future leaders of Fascism – but was absolutely the opposite of this latter mentality. If the war in Italy had been wanted and directed by a National Socialist Party, it is without a doubt that the diplomatic and *military* conduct of Italy would have been, primarily in its relations with the *Entente*, much different from what it was. And perhaps the European war would have ended much sooner and better, without America's intervention. Interventionism had to content itself with resisting socialist neutralism and defeatism and to fighting desperately against the weak liberal governments in order to prevent the war from ending in disaster, as the neutralists and socialists desired. If Salandra had brought Mussolini into power with him in May 1915, if, in a word, the government of 1915 had not remained a liberal ministry, but had been replaced by a revolutionary one, our affairs would have gone far better. The history of Italian, and, above all, Milanese, interventionist efforts, to avert Caporetto, is

---

[24]Original footnote: Whoever might wish to understand and delve more deeply into all this should read the prophetic book by MASSIMO ROCCA: *Dopo Tripoli e la guerra balcanica*, Lugano, 1913.

still little known. Nevertheless, we saw the war end with our victory. The democrats immediately raised the Adriatic question and broke interventionism apart. At *La Scala* in Milan, Bissolati had to be booed, painfully.

The democrats gained influence over the combatants. Mussolini, on the contrary, should have, before the start of the Paris Conference – and without the defection of the democrats and Nitti's pseudo-Machiavellian schemes, he could have – assumed the government by relying on the combatants from the trenches.

VI.

It is pointless to retell here the painful history of the Adriatic question. We did not conquer Rome, but, with D'Annunzio, Fiume. We arrived, God knows how, at the tenebrous elections of 1919. Eh, well: Mussolini who, already before Vittorio Veneto, had announced that it was necessary to march not *against* but *towards* labor, Mussolini who immediately after Vittorio Veneto imposed the rule of the eight-hour workday, Mussolini gave to the combatant Fasci, which had already been born, a program *for the elections* of 1919 that, far from being reactionary, was boldly and skillfully innovative and revolutionary.

If, therefore, all the dead and exhausted forces of Italy – and, at the forefront, the Socialist Party and all the social outcasts who consorted with it – had not been revitalized because of the Adriatic question, *we could have realized, as early as 1919, the revolution-*

ary spirit of Fascism. This latter, instead, finding itself face to face with an obscene Socialist revolution
sustained by the anti-Italian plutocratic governments
of the *Entente*, and not only tolerated but provoked
and protected by the Italian government, had to take,
as indeed it took, a necessarily reactive, repressive,
and rather *punitive* attitude. And this is what produced the reactionary appearance of Fascism in the
period that extended from the elections in November
of 1919 to the March on Rome.

VII.

Now, it is not quite accurate to assert that the restora-
tive period of Fascism is over. We are still quite far
from the end, and the path is still greatly encumbered.

If the Bolshevik revolution had come, the
work of reaction would have been easier and simpler.

Socialism has been negative. It has, if not destroyed, corrupted, ruined, decomposed everything.
Hence the necessity of restoring the values of the
past. We have had, it is true, a socialist revolution, but
a failed and not a victorious one. Hence, the enor-
mous ills of a *failed* revolution, without any of the ad-
vantages that every subversive revolution brings with
it. The immediate, and not yet terminated, task of Fascism is to reestablish energetically – as it does magnificently, by provoking the astonishment and admi-
ration of as many in the world [who] think, feel, and
understand – public order, the prestige of authority,
the treasure of the State, the traditional social organ-
isms that cannot be tampered with, in that they are sa-

cred and untouchable, the foremost among which are family and religion. But the rejuvenating soul exists and is imminent in Fascism. I believe I have demonstrated it in these historical notes. It will complete, on its own, the history of Italy and Europe.

– From *L'Italie nouvelle*, December 1923.

Other Books by the Publisher

Fanchette's Pretty Little Foot by Restif de la Bretonne

Je M'Accuse... by Léon Bloy

My Hospitals & My Prisons by Paul Verlaine

Salvation Through the Jews by Léon Bloy

Words of a Demolitions Contractor by Léon Bloy

Cellulely by Paul Verlaine

Ecclesiastical Laurels by Jacques Rochette de la Morlière

Flowers of Bitumen by Émile Goudeau

Songs for Her & Odes in Her Honor by Paul Verlaine

On Huysmans' Tomb by Léon Bloy

Ten Years a Bohemian by Émile Goudeau

The Soul of Napoleon by Léon Bloy

Blood of the Poor by Léon Bloy

Joan of Arc and Germany by Léon Bloy

A Platonic Love by Paul Alexis

The Revealer of the Globe: Christopher Columbus & His Future Beatification (Part One) by Léon Bloy

An Immodest Proposal by Dr. Helmut Schleppend

The Pornographer by Restif de la Bretonne

Style (Theory and History) by Ernest Hello

On the Threshold of the Apocalypse: 1913-1915 by Léon Bloy

She Who Weeps (Our Lady of La Salette) by Léon Bloy

The Sylph by Claude Prosper Jolyot de Crébillon (*fils*)

Voyage in France by a Frenchman by Paul Verlaine

Ourigan, Oregon by William Clark, Richard Robinson, and anonymous

Drowning by Yu Dafu

Cull of April by Francis Vielé-Griffin

The Misfortune of Monsieur Fraque by Paul Alexis

Fêtes Galantes & Songs Without Words by Paul Verlaine

Joys by Francis Vielé-Griffin

The Son of Louis XVI by Léon Bloy

Septentrion by Jean Raspail

The Resurrection of Villiers de l'Isle-Adam by Léon Bloy

Poems Saturnian by Paul Verlaine

The Biography of Léon Bloy: Memories of a Friend by René Martineau

Fredegund, France: A Book of Poetry by Richard Robinson

The Good Song by Paul Verlaine

Swans by Francis Vielé-Griffin

Constantinople and Byzantium by Léon Bloy

Enamels and Cameos by Théophile Gautier

Four Years of Captivity in Cochons-sur-Marne: 1900-1904 by Léon Bloy

Dark Minerva: Prolegomena: The Moral Construction of Dante's Divine Comedy by Giovanni Pascoli

What is Fascism: Discourses and Polemics by Giovanni Gentile

The Desperate Man by Léon Bloy

Meditations of a Solitary in 1916 by Léon Bloy

The Ride of Yeldis & Other Poems by Francis Vielé-Griffin

Silvie & The Chimeras by Gérard de Nerval

Italian Nationalism by Enrico Corradini

A Silver-Grey Death and *Drowning* by Yu Dafu

Doctrines of Hatred, Part I: Anti-Semitism by Anatole Leroy-Beaulieu

Rhymes of Joy by Théodore Hannon

Windows and Doors by Richard Robinson

The Perverted Peasant by Restif de la Bretonne

Early Poetry by Auguste de Villiers de l'Isle-Adam

Antisthenes: The Founder of Cynicism by Charles Chappuis

The Ungrateful Beggar by Léon Bloy

Great Men Are Slain Here by Léon Bloy

Fallacies: Part 3, Book 4 of Summa Logicae by William of Ockham